Publisher Inforn

30 Most Delicious Ke__ Vegetarian Diet Recipes

Author: Nisha Panchal

Before reading the book please read the disclaimer.

For further information, contact the author by email: info@BioMedArticles.com

Disclaimer

Every effort has been made to ensure that the information in this book in accurate and current at the time of publication. The author and the publisher cannot accept responsibility for any misuse or misunderstanding of any information contained herein, or any loss, damage or injury, be it health, financial or otherwise, suffered by any individual or group acting upon or relying on information contained herein.

The material and information in this book are for general information /educational purpose only. None of the opinions or suggestions in this book is intended as a substitute for medical advice and/or consultation with physician or technical expert. Before starting any diet, you should always consult with your physician to rule out any health issues that could arise. If you have concerns about your or your baby's health, please seek professional advice.

Table of Contents

INTRODUCTION

Ketogenic Vegetarian diets are generally rich in antioxidants, healthy fats and certain vitamins/minerals. Meat-based diets usually have higher levels of protein, iron, zinc, vitamin B12 and calcium.

Maintaining a healthy veggie diet means you need to understand the key principles of vegetarian nutrition. Healthy vegetarian or vegan diets are not complicated, however you need to be aware of the main principles of good nutrition.

Properly planned ketogenic vegetarian nutrition can far exceed the healthiness of most meat-based diets. Whilst a ketogenic vegetarian diet plan may seem boring to many people, it definitely does not need to be dull! There are so many fabulous recipes that you can follow, especially some ethnic dishes which are famous for their veggie and spicy ingredients.

One general misconception about ketogenic vegetarianism is that their diet does not provide enough protein or iron. This absolutely need not be true. Legumes, beans, grains, soy, nuts and seeds are great proteins sources. They also provide various antioxidants, vitamins, minerals and fibers which are not present in a meat-based diet. So a ketogenic vegetarian diet can actually be much healthier.

A veggie diet specifically designed for athletes or bodybuilders should contain the correct levels of proteins, carbohydrates, vitamins, minerals, proteins and good fats. However, like all kinds of dietary plans, if you are struggling with which type of a vegetarian planner is good for you, you should seek help from a healthy ketogenic vegetarian meal planner or dietician.

Ketogenic Vegetarian diet plans are a popular weight loss option, as many of the foods in the diet plan are low in cholesterol and fats. Anyone looking to lose weight needs to limit foods with high levels of bad fats and cholesterol, and therefore adopting a veggie diet planner will help to achieve this.

A good ketogenic meal planning system can benefit you in a variety of ways. Healthy vegetarian diet plans will be well balanced with a whole range of fruits, vegetables, whole grains and legumes. The plan should include a variety of foods in each food group, to be both balanced and to provide you with load of recipe options!

This eBook will provide you with a few delicious options quick and tasty recipes.

1. RASPBERRY ARUGULA SALAD

Prep Time: 5 minutes

Cook Time: 0 minutes

Servings: 2

Ingredients:

- 2 oz (57 g) arugula
- 1 oz (28 g) baby spinach
- 1 cucumber, chopped
- 10-15 parsley or cilantro leaves (remove the stem)
- 14 pitted olives
- Salt to taste
- 1 Tablespoon (15 ml) olive oil
- 1 Tablespoon (15 ml) lemon juice
- 14 raspberries

Directions:

1. Place all the ingredients into a salad bowl (excluding the raspberries) and toss well.
2. Add salt to taste.
3. Top with raspberries but don't mix in as they get crushed easily.

Nutritional Facts (Per serving):

- Calories: 114
- Sugar: 3g
- Fat: 9g
- Carbohydrates: 6g
- Fiber: 3g
- Protein: 2g

2. LASAGNA ROLLS

Prep Time: 20 mins

Cook Time: 20 mins

Total Time: 40 mins

Soaking Time: 8 hrs

Servings: 10

Ingredients:

Rolls:

- 1 eggplant
- 1 zucchini
- 1/2 cup organic tomato sauce
- 8 oz. cashew cheese recipe below
- 1 tsp ghee or coconut oil
- salt and pepper to taste

Cashew cheese:

- 1 cup raw cashews
- Enough water to cover the cashews
- Dash of sea salt

To add in after:

- 1/2 tsp garlic powder 1/2 tsp salt

Directions:

Directions for the cashew cheese:

1. Soak cashews in water and sea salt for 8-24 hours. You can leave it to soak overnight if you want.

2. Drain the water from the cashews. Put soaked cashews in a food processor or

strong blender (like Vitamix) along with garlic powder and salt.

3. Blend until creamy. If you want it to be a little thinner you can add a little more water. Store in a jar in the fridge.

Directions for lasagna bites:

1. Thinly slice the eggplant and zucchini lengthwise. Sprinkle salt over the slices and place salt side down on a paper towel. Sprinkle salt on the other side of the slices and let sit for about 10 minutes. This will draw the water out of the eggplant and zucchini.

2. Get another paper towel and dab the moisture off of the eggplant and zucchini until it's dry.

3. Heat oil in a skillet on high. Once the oil is hot, place the eggplant and zucchini slices in the pan for about 1-2 minutes on each side just to let it brown and cook a little. Set cooked slices aside until you've seared all of them.

4. Once they are all cooked, take one slice and put about 1 tbsp of the cashew cheese in the middle of the slice, then fold it over to cover the cheese and put on a plate. If you want, you can double wrap the cashew cheese with a slice of eggplant and a slice of zucchini or you can just do one slice for each, it's up to you.

5. Once all of the slices have been used take about 1 tsp of organic tomato sauce and drizzle over each roll. Sprinkle salt, pepper and herbs to taste and serve!

Nutritional Facts (Per serving):

Amount Per Serving (1 roll)

- Calories: 93 Calories from Fat 54% Daily Value
- Total Fat: 6g (9%)
- Saturated Fat: 1g (5%)
- Cholesterol: 1mg (0%)
- Sodium: 68mg (3%)
- Potassium: 281mg (8%)

- Total Carbohydrates: 7g (2%)
- Dietary Fiber: 2g (8%)
- Sugars: 3g
- Protein: 3g (6%)

3. LOW CARB FALAFEL WITH TAHINI SAUCE

Prep Time: 15 mins

Cook Time: 20

Total Time: 35 mins

Serving: (8) 3" patties

Ingredients:

- 1 cup raw cauliflower, pureed
- 1/2 cup ground slivered almonds
- 1 Tbsp ground cumin
- 1/2 Tbsp ground coriander
- 1 tsp kosher salt
- 1/2 tsp cayenne pepper
- 1 clove garlic, minced
- 2 Tbsp fresh parsley, chopped
- 2 large eggs
- 3 Tbsp coconut flour

Tahini sauce:

- 2 Tbsp tahini paste
- 3 Tbsp water
- 1 Tbsp lemon juice
- 1 clove garlic, minced
- 1/2 tsp kosher salt, more to taste if desired

Directions:

1. For the cauliflower you should end up with a cup of the puree. It takes about 1 medium head (florets only) to get that much. First chop it up with a knife, then add it to a food processor or magic bullet and pulse until it's blended but still has a grainy texture.

2. You can grind the almonds in a similar manner – just don't over grind them, you want the texture.

3. Combine the ground cauliflower and ground almonds in a medium bowl. Add the rest of the ingredients and stir until well blended.

4. Heat a half and half mix of olive and grapeseed (or any other light oil) oil until sizzling. While its heating, form the mix into 8 three-inch patties that are about the thickness of a hockey puck.

5. Fry them four at a time until browned on one side and then flip and cook the other side. Resist the urge to flip too soon – you should see the edges turning brown before you attempt it – maybe 4 minutes or so per side. Remove to a plate lined with a paper towel to drain any excess oil.

6. Serve with tahini sauce and a tomato & parsley garnish if desired.

Tahini sauce:

1. Blend all ingredients in a bowl.
2. Thin with more water if you like a lighter consistency.

Nutritional Facts (Per serving):

Serving Size: 2 patties

- Calories: 281
- Fat: 24g
- Carbohydrates: 5g net
- Protein: 8g

4. KALE AND BLUEBERRY SALAD

Prep Time: 5 mins

Cook Time: 0 minutes

Servings: 2

Ingredients:

- 6 oz (170 g) kale, chopped roughly
- 10 blueberries
- 1 Tablespoon (4 g) sliced almonds [use coconut flakes for AIP]
- 1/4 red onion, cut into thin slices
- 1 Tablespoon (2 g) parsley
- 1 Tablespoon (15 ml) lemon juice
- 2 Tablespoons (30 ml) olive oil
- Salt and pepper to taste

Directions:

1. Toss all the ingredients together.
2. Divide between 2 plates and serve.

Nutritional Facts

Serving Size: 1 plate

- Calories: 191
- Sugar: 2g Fat: 16g
- Carbohydrates: 13g
- Fiber: 4g
- Protein: 4g

5. ZUCCHINI NOODLES WITH AVOCADO SAUCE

Prep Time: 10 mins

Total Time: 10 mins

Serving: 2

Ingredients

- 1 zucchini
- 1 1/4 cup basil (30 g)
- 1/3 cup water (85 ml)
- 4 tbsp pine nuts
- 2 tbsp lemon juice
- 1 avocado
- 12 sliced cherry tomatoes

Directions:

1. Make the zucchini noodles using a peeler or the Spiralizer.

2. Blend the rest of the ingredients (except the cherry tomatoes) in a blender until smooth.

3. Combine noodles, avocado sauce and cherry tomatoes in a mixing bowl.

4. These zucchini noodles with avocado sauce are better fresh, but you can store them in the fridge for 1 to 2 days.

Nutritional Facts (Per serving):

Serving Size: 1/2 of the recipe

- Calories: 313
- Sugar: 6.5g
- Sodium: 22mg
- Fat: 26.8g
- Saturated Fat: 3.1g
- Carbohydrates: 18.7g
- Fiber: 9.7g
- Protein: 6.8g

6. VEGETARIAN KETO BURGERS

Prep Time: 15 minutes

Total Time: 20 minutes

Servings: 2

Ingredients:

Makes Marinated & grilled mushrooms:

- 2 medium-large flat mushrooms such as Portobello (150 g / 5.3 oz)
- 1 tbsp ghee or coconut oil (you can make your own)
- 1-2 tbsp freshly chopped basil or 1 tsp dried
- 1 tbsp freshly chopped oregano or 1/2 tsp dried
- 1 clove garlic, crushed
- 1/4 tsp salt or more to taste
- freshly ground black pepper

Serve with:

- 2 keto buns
- 2 tbsp mayonnaise - you can make your own
- 2 large eggs, free-range or organic
- 2 slices hard cheese such as cheddar or gouda (40 g / 1.4 oz)
- 1 cup mixed lettuce

Directions:

1. Make the Ultimate Keto Buns. Prepare the mushrooms for marinating. Season

with salt and pepper, add crushed garlic and freshly chopped herbs and ghee, preferably melted. Keep some of the ghee for frying the eggs. Keep the mushrooms at room temperature and marinate for up to an hour. Although marinating is highly recommended, you can skip it if you don't have time.

2. Place the mushrooms top side up on a hot griddle pan or a regular pan. Cook over a medium-high heat for about 5 minutes. Then, flip on the other side and cook for 5 more minutes.

3. Take off the heat. Flip back on the top side and top each of the mushrooms with cheese slices. Just before serving, place under a broiler for a few minutes until the cheese has melted.

4. Meanwhile, fry the eggs on the remaining ghee. I used these molds to create perfect shapes for the burgers. Cook the eggs until the egg white is opaque and the yolks still runny. Then, take off the heat.

5. Cut the buns in half and place each half, cut side down on a hot griddle pan and cook for 2-3 minutes until crispy.

6. Start assembling the burgers by adding a tablespoon of mayo on each of the keto bun halves. Top with portobello mushrooms.

7. Fried eggs a slices of tomato and lettuce. Serve any remaining lettuce aside. Enjoy!

Nutritional Facts (Per serving):

- Calories: 637
- Total Carbs: 18.8g
- Fiber: 10.1g
- Net Carbs: 8.7g
- Protein: 23.7g
- Fat: 55.1g
- Saturated: 18.9g

7. CRISPY PEANUT TOFU & CAULIFLOWER RICE STIR-FRY

Prep Time: 30 minutes

Cook Time: 1 hour

Total Time: 1 hour 30 minutes

Servings: 2

Ingredients:

STIR-FRY

- 12 ounces extra-firm tofu (organic & non-GMO if possible)
- 1 Tbsp toasted sesame oil
- 1 small head cauliflower
- 2 cloves garlic (minced 2 cloves yield ~1 Tbsp or 6 g)

SAUCE

- 1 1/2 Tbsp toasted sesame oil
- 1/4 cup low sodium soy sauce (tamari for GF eaters)
- 1/4 cup light brown sugar (or honey if not vegan)
- 1/2 tsp chili garlic sauce
- 2 1/2 Tbsp peanut butter or almond butter (natural, salted)

OPTIONAL EXTRAS

1. Veggies: baby bok choy, green onion, red pepper, broccoli
2. Toppings: fresh lime juice, cilantro, sriracha

Directions:

1. Begin by draining tofu 1.5 hours before you want your meal ready. If your block of tofu is larger than 12 ounces, trim it down. You don't need a full pound for this recipe (see notes).

2. Roll tofu in an absorbent towel several times and then place something heavy on top to press. I use a pot on top of a cutting board and sometimes add something to the pot to add more weight. Do this for 15 minutes.

3. Near the end of draining, preheat oven to 400 degrees F (204 C) and cube tofu. Place on a parchment-lined baking sheet and arrange in a single layer. Bake for 25 minutes to dry/firm the tofu. Once baked, remove from oven and let cool.

4. Prepare sauce by whisking together ingredients until combined. Taste and adjust flavor as needed. You can add a little more sweetener and peanut butter.

5. Add cooled tofu to the sauce and stir to coat. Let marinate for at least 15

minutes to saturate the tofu and infuse the flavor.

6. In the meantime, shred your cauliflower into rice by using a large grater or food processor. You don't want it too fine, just somewhat close to the texture of rice. Set aside. Mince garlic if you haven't already done so, and prepare any veggies you want to add to the dish (optional).

7. Heat a large skillet over medium to medium-high heat (6 out of 10), and if adding any veggies to your dish, cook them now in a bit of sesame oil and a dash of soy sauce. Remove from pan and set aside and cover to keep warm.

8. Use a slotted spoon to spoon tofu into the preheated pan. Add a few spoonfuls of the sauce to coat. Cook, stirring frequently for a few minutes until browned. It will stick to the pan a bit, so don't worry. Remove from pan and set aside and cover to keep warm.

9. Rinse your pan under very hot water and scrape away any residue. Place back on oven.

10. Add a drizzle of sesame oil to the pan, then add garlic and cauliflower rice and stir. Put cover on to steam the "rice." Cook for about 5-8 minutes until slightly browned and tender, stirring occasionally. Then add a few spoonfuls of sauce to season and stir.

11. Place cauliflower rice and top with veggies and tofu. Serve with any leftover sauce. Leftovers reheat well and will keep covered in the fridge for up to a couple days.

Nutritional Facts (Per serving):

- Calories: 524
- Fat: 34g
- Saturated fat: 5g
- Sodium: 1400mg
- Carbohydrates: 38.5g
- Fiber: 7g
- Sugar: 24.7g
- Protein: 24.5g

8. KETO KALE TATOR TOTS

Prep Time: 15 minutes

Cook Time: 1 hour

Total Time: 1 hour 15 minutes

Servings: 8 people

Ingredients:

- 6 cups water
- 2 lb cauliflower remove leaves and cut into florets
- 2 tablespoon garlic powder
- 1 teaspoon sea salt
- 1/3 cup coconut flour
- 3 large eggs
- 1 Tablespoon Dr Cowan Kale Powder

Directions:

1. Place the water in a large pan and bring to a boil, add the cauliflower and let cook for 4 minutes.

2. Drain and let cool completely. Finely dice the cauliflower. Please note: You do NOT want to use your food processor because it will make a puree which won't work for this recipe.

3. Add the diced cauliflower, coconut flour, the spices, and kale powder to a large bowl and mix.

4. Finally add the eggs and mix until well blended

5. Scoop out a large spoonful and shape into tots. Place on a baking pan lined with parchment paper.

6. Place in your oven at 350 degrees for 55 -60 minutes and serve with a hot sauce. Your final product should be more golden than the photo, so don't worry if they are more browned - it just makes them taste better in my opinion.

Nutritional Facts (Per serving):

- Calories: 52 Calories from Fat 18% Daily Value
- Total Fat: 2g (3%)
- Saturated Fat: 1g (5%)
- Cholesterol: 61mg (20%)
- Sodium: 335mg (14%)
- Potassium: 55mg (2%)
- Total Carbohydrates: 4g (1%)
- Dietary Fiber: 1g (4%)
- Sugars: 0g
- Protein: 3g (6%)

9. BALSAMIC SHALLOT MUSHROOMS

Prep Time: 5 minutes

Cook Time: 15 minutes

Total Time: 20 minutes

Serving: 6

Ingredients:

- 3 tablespoons salted butter
- 1 large shallot, thinly sliced
- 1-pound cremini mushrooms
- 1/4 cup beef stock
- 1/4 cup balsamic vinegar
- 2 tablespoons chopped fresh flat-leaf parsley
- 1 sprig fresh thyme, leaves picked
- sea salt and black pepper, to taste

Directions:

1. Heat a large skillet over medium heat. Add the butter and shallot. Sauté until the shallots are tender and translucent – about 3 to 5 minutes.

2. To the pan, add the mushrooms, beef stock, balsamic vinegar, parsley and thyme. Increase heat to medium-high, bring to a boil, and then the reduce heat to low and let simmer for 8 to 10 minutes, or until the mushrooms are tender and the sauce has reduced.

3. Taste, and add salt, and pepper, if desired.

Nutritional Facts (Per serving):

- Calories: 89
- Fat: 6g
- Carbohydrates: 6g
- Fiber: 1g
- Protein: 3g

10. CREAMY ASPARAGUS MASH

Prep Time: 10 minutes

Cook Time: 5 minutes

Servings: 2

Ingredients:

- 10 asparagus shoots, chopped and blanched (2 min)
- 1/4 onion, diced and cooked in coconut oil
- 2 Tablespoons coconut cream
- 2 Tablespoons fresh parsley
- 1 teaspoon lemon juice
- 1/2 teaspoon salt (or to taste)
- Dash of pepper (omit for AIP)

Directions:

1. Saute the diced onions in coconut oil until they turn translucent.

2. Blanch the asparagus pieces in boiling water for 2 minutes and drain immediately.

3. Place the sautéed onions, blanched asparagus, coconut cream, parsley, lemon juice, and salt and pepper into a blender.

4. Blend really well. Serve warm or cold.

Nutritional Facts (Per serving):

- Calories: 70
- Sugar: 2g
- Fat: 6g
- Carbohydrates: 4g
- Fiber: 2g
- Protein: 2g

11. VEGETARIAN KETO PIZZA

Prep Time: 15 minutes

Cook Time: 15 minutes

Servings: 4

Ingredients:

For the keto pizza crust:

- 1/2 cup (60 g) almond flour
- 2 Tablespoons (14 g) flax meal
- 1 Tablespoon (2 g) nutritional yeast
- 1 Tablespoons (15 ml) olive oil
- 1 egg, whisked
- Salt and pepper, to taste

For the pizza toppings:

- 1/4 cup (60 ml) Keto pizza sauce
- 2 Tablespoons (30 ml) cashew butter
- 1 Tablespoon (2 g) nutritional yeast
- 6 basil leaves, chopped

Directions:

1. Preheat oven to 400 F (200 C).

2. Mix all the base ingredients together to form a dough. Roll out into a round flat pizza crust.

3. Bake for 15 minutes, carefully flipping the crust after 10 minutes.

4. Mix the pizza sauce and cashew butter together. Spread on top of the pizza crust.

5. Sprinkle chopped basil on top.

Nutritional Facts (Per serving):

- Calories: 198
- Sugar: 2g
- Fat: 16g
- Carbohydrates: 8g
- Fiber: 4g
- Protein: 8g

12. KETO GARLIC BREAD

Prep Time: 10 mins

Cook Time: 50 minutes

Servings: 20

Ingredients:

Bread

- 1¼ cups almond flour
- 5 tbsp ground psyllium husk powder
- 2 tsp baking powder
- 1 tsp sea salt
- 2 tsp cider vinegar or white wine vinegar
- 1 cup boiling water
- 3 egg whites

Garlic butter

- 4 oz. butter, at room temperature
- 1 garlic clove, minced
- 2 tbsp fresh parsley, finely chopped
- ½ tsp salt

Directions:

1. Preheat the oven to 350°F (175°C). Mix the dry ingredients in a bowl.

2. Bring the water to a boil and add this, the vinegar and egg whites to the bowl, while whisking with a hand mixer for about 30 seconds. Don't overmix the dough, the consistency should resemble Play-Doh.

3. Form with moist hands into 10 pieces and roll into hot dog buns. Make sure to leave enough space between them on the baking sheet to double in size.

4. Bake on lower rack in oven for 40-50 minutes, they're done when you can hear a hollow sound when tapping the bottom of the bun.

5. Make the garlic butter while the bread is baking. Mix all the ingredients together and put in the fridge.

6. Take the buns out of the oven when they're done and leave to let cool. Take the garlic butter out of the fridge. When the buns are cooled, cut them in halves, using a serrated knife, and spread garlic butter on each half.

7. Turn your oven up to 425°F (225°C) and bake the garlic bread for 10-15 minutes, until golden brown.

Nutritional Facts (Per serving):

- Calories: 92
- Net carbs: 1g (3%)
- Fiber: 2g
- Fat: 9g (88%)
- Protein: 2g (9%)

13. WHOLE30 PAN ROASTED PORTOBELLO EGG "TOAST"

Prep Time: 25 mins

Cook Time: 25 minutes

Servings: 4

Ingredients:

- 2 portobello mushrooms
- 4 medium/small tomatoes
- 4 eggs
- fresh thyme for sprinkling in top
- salt & pepper to taste
- olive oil for cooking
- 6-8 cloves garlic

Directions:

1. Slice the portobello mushrooms in half. Drizzle a large fry pan with olive oil. Place the mushrooms in the pan and cook for about 10 minutes over medium heat on the stovetop (about 5 minutes on each side) until soft and kinda crispy on the edges. Once the mushrooms are cooked set them aside.

2. Cut tomatoes in half and cook in the fry pan with a drizzle of olive oil (enough olive oil so they don't stick or burn). Cook for about 10 minutes (about 5 minutes on each side). Once the tomatoes are cooked remove them from the pan and set aside.

3. Mince garlic and sauté with a drizzle of olive oil for about 1 minute until golden and crispy. Then set aside.

4. Fry the eggs (to your liking). Then layer and assemble the mushroom "toast". Top with crispy garlic, fresh thyme leaves, sea salt, and fresh cracked pepper.

Nutritional Facts (Per serving):

- Calories: 162 Calories from Fat 108% Daily Value
- Total Fat: 12g (18%)
- Saturated Fat: 2g (10%)
- Cholesterol: 186mg (62%)
- Total Carbohydrates: 8g (3%)
- Dietary Fiber: 1g (4%)
- Sugars: 4g
- Protein: 8g (16%)

14. SALAD SANDWICHES

Prep Time: 5 mins

Cook Time: 0 minutes

Serving: 1

Ingredients:

- 2 oz. Romaine lettuce or baby gem lettuce
- ½ oz. butter
- 1 oz. edam cheese or other cheese of your liking
- ½ avocado
- 1 cherry tomatoes

Directions:

1. Rinse the lettuce thoroughly and use as a base for the toppings.

2. Smear butter on the lettuce leaves and slice the cheese, avocado and tomato and add on top.

Nutritional Facts (Per serving)

- Calories: 374
- Net carbs: 3 g (4 %)
- Fiber: 8 g
- Fat: 34 g (85%)
- Protein: 10 g (11%)

15. MEDITERRANEAN ROASTED CABBAGE STEAKS WITH BASIL PESTO & FETA

Prep time: 5 mins

Cook time: 20 mins

Total time: 25 mins

Servings: 3

Ingredients:

- 1 Small Head Cabbage, sliced into "steaks"
- 4 oz Basil Pesto
- 1 cup Shredded Parmesan Cheese
- 2 oz Feta Cheese, crumbled
- 2 small Tomatoes, sliced
- 5-6 Marinated Artichoke halves
- 1 tbsp Mediterranean Seasoning
- Fresh Basil, to garnish
- OPTIONAL TOPPINGS include olives, mozzarella, mushrooms, roasted red pepper, etc.

Directions:

1. Heat oven to 400 and spray a large sheet pan with nonstick spray.

2. Arrange the cabbage in a single layer on the sheet pan so the edges are all touching. Slather pesto on the steak halves and be generous as a lot will melt into the cabbage folds.

3. Top with cheese and tomato and bake until the edges of the cabbage are crisp and all of the cheese is bubbly, about 20 minutes.

4. Sprinkle with Seasoning and Basil. Serve HOT with an extra scoop of Pesto for dipping!

Nutritional Facts (Per serving)

- Calories: 200
- Fat: 11.5g (of which 4g saturates)
- Carbohydrates: 15g
- Fiber: 7g
- Protein: 9g

16. LOW-CARB EGG STUFFED AVOCADO

Prep Time: 5 mins

Cook Time: 15 minutes

Servings: 2

Ingredients:

- 1 extra large or 2 medium avocados, seed removed (300 g / 10.6 oz)
- 4 large eggs, free-range or organic
- 1/4 cup mayonnaise (you can make your own) (58 g / 2 oz)
- 2 tbsp sour cream or cream cheese or more mayo for dairy-free (24 g / 0.8 oz)
- 1 tsp Dijon mustard (you can make your own)
- 2 medium spring onions (30 g / 1.1 oz)
- 1/4 tsp salt or more to taste (I used pink Himalayan)
- freshly ground black pepper to taste

Directions:

1. Start by cooking the eggs. Fill a small saucepan with water up to three quarters. Add a good pinch of salt. This will prevent the eggs from cracking. Bring to a boil. Using a spoon or hand, dip each egg in and out of the boiling water - be careful not to get burnt. This will prevent the egg from cracking as the temperature change won't be so dramatic. To get the eggs hard-boiled, you need round 10 minutes. This timing works for large eggs. When done,

remove from the heat and place in a bowl filled with cold water. I like and always use this egg timer!

2. Dice the eggs and finely slice the spring onion.

3. In a bowl, mix the diced eggs, mayo, sour cream, Dijon mustard and spring onion - leave some spring onion for garnish. Season with salt and pepper to taste.

4. Scoop the middle of the avocado out leaving 1/2 - 1 inch of the avocado flesh. Cut the scooped avocado into small pieces.

5. Place the chopped avocado into the bowl with eggs and mix until well combined.

6. Fill each avocado half with the egg & avocado mixture and top with more spring onion.

Nutritional Facts (Per serving):

- Calories: 616
- Total Carbs: 15.3 g
- Fiber: 10.6 g
- Net Carbs: 4.8 g
- Protein: 16.5 g
- Fat: 56.8 g of which Saturated 11 g

17. LOW CARB VEGAN COCONUT LIME NOODLES WITH CHILI TAMARI TOFU

Prep Time: 5 mins

Cook Time: 0 minutes

Servings: 4

Ingredients:

- For the Noodles
- 1 can (13.5oz/400ml) Full fat coconut milk
- 2 packages (8oz/226g each) shirataki noodles
- 4 tbsp sesame seeds
- juice and zest of 1 lime
- 1/2 tsp ground or fresh grated ginger
- 1/4 tsp red pepper flakes
- pinch of salt

For the Tofu

- 1 block (13.5oz/397g) extra firm tofu
- 4 tbsp low sodium tamari
- 1 tbsp olive oil
- 1/4 tsp cayenne pepper (or ground chili pepper of choice)

Directions:

1. Preheat your oven to 350F.

2. Drain tofu, and press out excess moisture. Cube into roughly 1"x1" blocks.

3. Mix together tamari, olive oil and cayenne. In a shallow dish, arrange the tofu cubes in a single layer, and pour the mixture over the tofu. You'll want to flip the pieces a few times so that they are evenly covered.

4. Place the tofu pieces on a baking sheet and bake for 20-25 minutes.

5. While the tofu is baking, drain and rinse the noodles. Add to a pan on medium heat, along with the rest of the noodle ingredients and mix until well combined. Partially cover and cook for about 10 minutes, then reduce the heat and continue cooking for another 10 minutes.

6. Once the tofu is done, turn off the heat under the noodles as well. Then let everything cool for a few minutes before plating. Garnish with lime zest, red pepper flakes, microgreens, more sesame seeds, or whatever your heart desires.

Nutritional Facts (Per Serving):

- Calories: 374.3 (19%)
- Total Fat: 31.1g (48%)
- Saturated Fat: 18.5g (93%)
- Cholesterol: 0mg (0%)
- Total Carbohydrates: 9.1g (3%)
- Dietary Fiber: 3.6g (15%)
- Sugars: 2.4g
- Protein: 15.7g (31%)

18. CURRIED CAULIFLOWER RICE KALE SOUP

Prep Time: 30 minutes

Cook Time: 20 minutes

Total Time: 50 minutes

Servings: 4

Ingredients:

- 5-6 cups of cauliflower florets (about 3-4 cups when "riced"). See notes.
- 2- 3 tbsp curry powder or curry seasoning (turmeric should is usually included in the curry seasoning/powder)
- 1 tsp garlic powder
- 1/2 tsp cumin
- 1/2 tsp paprika
- 1/4 tsp sea salt
- 2-3 tbsp olive oil for roasting
- 3/4 cup red onion chopped
- 1 tsp minced garlic
- 2 tsp olive oil or avocado oil
- 8 kale leaves with stems removed and chopped
- 2 cups (5oz) chopped carrots
- 4 cups broth (vegetable or chicken if not vegan)
- 1 cup almond milk or coconut milk (the drinking kind works best and is smoother).
- 1/2 tsp red pepper or chili flakes (use less if you don't want as spicy)
- 1/2 tsp black pepper
- salt to taste after cooked.

Directions:

1. preheat oven to 400F.

2. In a small bowl, toss your cauliflower florets with the curry powder, garlic powder, cumin, paprika, salt, and 3 tbsp oil.

3. Spread the cauliflower florets on a baking dish or roasting pan. Place in oven and roast for 20 -22 minutes until tender but not overcooked. slightly under cooked.

4. Remove and set aside.

5. While the cauliflower is cooling, prep the rest of your veggies but chopping them up on cutting board.

6. Next place cauliflower florets in a Food Processor or blender and pulse a few times until the cauliflower is chopped or "riced." See picture in post.

7. Once all the cauliflower is riced and kale/veggies are chopped, prepare your cooking pot.

8. Place onion, 2 tsp oil, and minced garlic in large stock pot. Sautee for 5 minutes until fragant.

9. Next add in your broth, milk, veggies, cauliflower "rice," and the red chili pepper and black pepper.

10. Bring to a quick boil (make sure milk does get too hot), then simmer for another 20 minutes or so until veggies are all cooked.

11. Add dash of sea salt if desired once ready to serve.

12. Garnish with herbs and nut/seed crackers crumbles.

Nutritional Facts (Per serving):

Serving Size: 1 bowl

- Calories: 162
- Sugar: 6g
- Sodium: 250mg
- Fat: 8g
- Saturated Fat: 1.3g

- Unsaturated Fat: 0
- Trans Fat: 0
- Carbohydrates: 20g
- Fiber: 9g
- Protein: 6g
- Cholesterol: 0mg

19. CREAMY LEMON GREEN BEANS

Prep Time: 10 mins

Cook Time: 15 minutes

Servings: 4

Ingredients:

- 10 oz. fresh green beans
- 3 oz. butter or olive oil
- ½ tsp sea salt
- ¼ tsp ground black pepper
- 1 cup heavy whipping cream
- ½ lemon, the zest
- ½ cup fresh parsley (optional)

Directions:

1. Trim and rinse the green beans.

2. Heat butter or oil in a frying pan.

3. Sauté the beans for 3-4 minutes over medium-high heat until they begin to brown. Lower the heat towards the end. Salt and pepper to taste.

4. Add heavy cream and let simmer for 1-2 minutes. Grate the lemon zest finely and sprinkle on top of the green beans before serving. (Or, you can use a knife to cut very thin strips of zest—yellow part only—and add to the dish.)

5. Add finely chopped parsley before serving.

Nutritional Facts (Per serving):

- Calories: 391
- Net carbs: 5g (5%)
- Fiber: 2g
- Fat: 40g (91%)
- Protein: 3g (3%)

20. PERFECT SPINACH & FETA OMELET

Prep Time: 15 mins

Cook Time: 0 minutes

Serving: 1

Ingredients:

- 3 large eggs, free-range or organic
- 1 clove garlic
- 1 cup white mushrooms, sliced (70 g / 2.5 oz)
- 3 cups spinach, fresh (90 g / 3.2 oz) or 2/3 cup frozen and thawed (100 g / 3.5 oz)
- 1/3 cup feta cheese, crumbled (50 g / 1.8 oz)
- 2 tbsp ghee (30 g / 1.1 oz)
- salt and pepper to taste (I like pink Himalayan salt)

Directions:

1. First, prepare the filling. Peel and finely dice the garlic and place on a pan greased with a tablespoon of ghee. Season with salt and cook over a medium-high heat for just a minute until fragrant. Add the sliced mushrooms and cook for 5 minutes until lightly browned stirring occasionally.

2. Add the spinach and cook until wilted for just a minute or two (squeeze out the water if using frozen and thawed spinach). Take off the heat and place in

a bowl. Discard the excess liquids before using the pan for cooking the omelet.

3. Crack the eggs into a bowl and mix using a fork. Season with salt and pepper to taste.

4. Pour the eggs evenly in a hot pan greased with a tablespoon of ghee. Use a spatula to bring in the egg from the sides towards to centre for the first 30 seconds. Tilt the pan as needed to cover it with the eggs. Lower the heat and cook for another minute. Don't rush it and don't try to cook it fast or the omelet will end up being too crispy and dry. The desired texture should be soft and fluffy.

5. When the top is almost cooked, add the spinach and mushroom topping and crumbled feta. Fold the omelet in half, cook for another minute just to warm up the topping and slide on a serving plate.

6. Enjoy!

Nutritional Facts (Per serving):

- Calories: 659
- Total carbs: 9.7g
- Fiber: 2.8g
- Net carbs: 7g
- Protein: 30.9g
- Fat: 55.5g

21. VEGETARIAN LETTUCE WRAPS

Prep Time: 10 mins

Cook Time: 15 mins

Total Time: 25 mins

Servings: 4

Ingredients:

- 3 tablespoons hoisin sauce
- 3 tablespoons reduced-sodium soy sauce
- 2 tablespoons rice vinegar
- 1 teaspoon sesame oil
- 2 teaspoons canola oil — or grapeseed oil
- 1 package extra-firm tofu — (12- to 14-ounces), do not use silken
- 8 ounces baby bella cremini mushrooms — finely chopped
- 1 can water chestnuts — (8 ounces), drained and finely chopped
- 2 cloves garlic — minced
- 2 teaspoons freshly grated ginger
- 1/4 teaspoon red pepper flakes — omit if sensitive to spice
- 4 green onions — thinly sliced, divided
- 8 large inner leaves romaine lettuce — from a romaine heart or butter lettuce leaves
- Optional for serving: grated carrots — additional red pepper flakes

Directions:

1. In a small bowl, stir together the hoisin, soy sauce, rice vinegar, and sesame oil. Set aside.

2. Press the tofu between paper towels to squeeze out as much liquid as possible. Refresh the paper towels and press again. Heat the 2 teaspoons canola oil in a large nonstick skillet over medium-high. Once the oil is hot, crumble in the tofu, breaking it into very small pieces as it cooks. Continue cooking for 5 minutes, then add the diced mushrooms. Continue cooking until any remaining tofu liquid cooks off and the tofu starts to turn golden, about 3 minutes more. Stir in the water chestnuts, garlic, ginger, red pepper flakes, and half of the green onions and cook until fragrant, about 30 seconds more.

3. Pour the sauce over the top of the tofu mixture and stir to coat. Cook just until you hear bubbling and the sauce is warmed through, 30 to 60 seconds.

4. Spoon the tofu mixture into individual lettuce leaves. Top with remaining green onions, grated carrots, and additional red pepper flakes as desired. Enjoy immediately.

Nutritional Facts (Per serving):

- Calories: 194
- Fat: 9g, Saturated Fat: 1g
- Sodium: 612mg
- Carbohydrates: 16g
- Fiber: 14g

22. VEGETARIAN KETO LASAGNA

Prep Time: 20-25 mins

Cook Time: 15 mins

Total Time: 1 hour

Servings: 6

Ingredients:

- 2 medium eggplants / aubergines (750 g / 26.5 oz / 1.6 lb)
- 1 cup Marinara sauce (240 g / 8.5 oz)
- 300 g fresh spinach (10.6 oz) or g frozen spinach (330 g / 11.6 oz)
- 1 1/3 cup feta cheese (200 g / 7.1 oz)
- 1 cup mozzarella cheese, grated (110 g / 4 oz)
- 1/2 cup parmesan cheese, grated (30 g / 1.1 oz)
- 6 large eggs, free-range or organic
- 1/4 cup + 2 tbsp ghee - you can make your own (85 g / 3 oz)
- 1/2 tsp salt or more to taste
- Optional: fresh herbs such as basil and oregano for garnish

Directions:

1. Preheat the oven to 200°C/400 °F. Slice the eggplant into 1/2 inch (~ 1 cm) slices and place on a baking tray. Grease with 1/4 of melted ghee, season with a pinch of salt and place in the oven. Cook for about 20 minutes.

2. If you're using frozen spinach, let it defrost at room temperature for a

couple of hours (or microwave). If you're using fresh spinach, you'll need to blanch it. Bring a pot of water to a boil over high heat. Fill a bowl with ice and water or simply with cold water. Place the spinach leaves into the boiling water and cook for 30-60 seconds. Transfer the leaves immediately into the iced water using tongs or a strainer. One it cools down, remove from the cold water. Drain the excess water by placing the spinach in a strainer and squeezing the excess fluids out.

3. Meanwhile, prepare the Marinara sauce by following this recipe.

4. When the eggplant is done, remove from the oven and set aside. Reduce the temperature to 180 °C/ 360 °F. Prepare the omelettes. Crack one egg at a time in a bowl, season with a pinch of salt and mix well.

5. Pour on in a hot pan greased with ghee (use the remaining 2 tablespoons of ghee for greasing the pan as needed) and swirl around to create a very thin omelette. Cook for just about a minute

or two, until the top is firm. Place on a plate and repeat for the remaining eggs. Make a total of 6 omelettes. Start assembling the lasagna by placing a layer of 2 omelettes on the bottom of a banking dish (I used a 9 x 12 inch / 23 x 30 cm baking dish).

6. You can create less layers if you like - it's totally up to you. Just make sure you top the lasagna with some mozzarella and parmesan.

7. Spread a third of the Marinara sauce on top of the omelettes. Add a third of the eggplant slices.

8. a third of the grated mozzarella cheese, half of the spinach.

9. and half of the crumbled feta cheese. Top with 2 more omelettes.

10. Repeat layering the lasagna: Spread a third of the Marinara sauce on top, add a third of the eggplant slices and a third of grated mozzarella. Add the remaining spinach and feta cheese. For the last layer, add the remaining omelettes,

marinara sauce, eggplant slices and mozzarella cheese. Top with all of the grated parmesan cheese and place in the oven. Bake for 25-30 minutes. When done, the top gets crispy and golden brown. Remove from the oven and set aside to cool down. Cut into 6 pieces / servings. Vegetarian Keto Lasagna Eat immediately or let it cool down and store in the fridge for up to 5 days. The lasagna can be served either warm or cold.

Nutritional Facts (Per serving):

- Calories: 190 Calories from Fat 131% Daily Value
- Total Fat: 14.6g (22%)
- Saturated Fat: 8.3g (42%)
- Total Carbohydrates: 2.1g (1%)
- Sugars: 0.6g
- Protein: 13.3g (27%)

23. KETO AND DAIRY-FREE VEGETABLE PIE

Prep Time: 30 mins

Cook Time: 30 mins

Total Time: 1 hour

Servings: 4

Ingredients:

- ¾ cup sunflower seeds
- 1 tbsp sesame seeds
- ¾ cup coconut flour
- 4 eggs
- 5 oz. melted butter
- 1 tbsp ground psyllium husk powder
- 1 tsp salt

Filling

- 51/3 oz. zucchini
- 3 oz. carrots
- 8 eggs
- 1¼ cups mayonnaise
- 1 tbsp dried parsley
- 1 tsp onion powder
- salt and pepper

Serving

- 7 oz. lettuce
- 4 tbsp olive oil
- ½ tbsp red wine vinegar
- salt and pepper

Directions:

1. Mix the sunflower and sesame seeds into a coarse flour in a food processor. Add the rest of the ingredients for the dough and mix until evenly combined. Take the dough out, form it to a ball and flatten it.

2. Cover in plastic wrap and put in the fridge for 30 minutes or more. Feel free to make the dough ahead of time and freeze it.

3. Preheat your oven to 400°F (200°C). Divide the dough evenly into as many pieces as you want servings.

4. Roll out each piece between two baking sheets or press out directly with oiled fingers into serving-sized baking dishes that are about 5-6 inches (13-15 cm) across. Pre-bake the crust for 5-7 minutes. Remove from oven.

5. Next, prepare the filling. Mix eggs, mayonnaise and spices well. Peel carrots and slice thinly, lengthwise. Rinse the zucchini (do not peel) and slice thinly, lengthwise.

6. Roll the slices like flowers and arrange in the pre-baked pie shells. Pour the egg mix over and bake at 350°F (175°C) for about 20-25 minutes, until set and golden brown.

7. Mix oil, salt, pepper and vinegar into a vinaigrette. Drizzle it over the salad and serve with the pie.

Nutritional Facts (Per serving):

- Calories: 1299
- Net carbs: 10g (3 %)
- Fiber: 17 g
- Fat: 124g (88 %)
- Protein: 29g (9 %)

24. KETO GARLIC GNOCCHI

Prep Time: 10 minutes

Cook Time: 25 minutes

Total Time: 35 minutes

Servings: 2

Ingredients:

- 2 cups shredded Mozzarella (Low-Moisture Part-Skim this is a MUST–otherwise it will fall apart when boiled! I find Kraft to work the best!)
- 3 egg yolks
- 1 tsp granulated garlic
- butter & olive oil for sauteing

Directions:

1. Place cheese and garlic in a microwave safe bowl and toss around to combine. Melt cheese in microwave for about 1 to 1 1/2 minutes.

2. Fold in one egg yolk at a time until a homogeneous dough forms. This actually takes a little elbow grease!

3. Portion dough into 4 balls.

4. Chill in refrigerator for at least 10 minutes.

5. Lightly grease a silpat or parchment (and your hands-it helps from sticking!) and roll out each ball into a 14-15" log.

6. Slice each log into 1" pieces. (If you like, you can press the tip of a fork onto each piece to get that "gnocchi" look but it's not necessary)

7. In a large pot, bring about a half gallon of salted water to a boil (like you would for normal pasta). Place all the gnocchi into the pot and cook until they float, about 2-3 minutes. The strain into a colander. (*note: a few of my readers say that have skipped this step and the gnocchi still turns out great!)

8. Heat a large non-stick pan on medium-high heat. Add a tablespoon of butter and a tablespoon of oil to pan.

9. Add gnocchi and saute each side for about 1-2 minutes, until golden brown.

10. Season with salt and pepper and serve!

Nutritional Facts (Per serving):

- Calories: 1023
- Net carbs: 10g (4%)
- Fiber: 6g
- Fat: 93g (83%)
- Protein: 33g (13%)

25. KETO MUSHROOM AND CHEESE FRITTATA

Prep Time: 15 mins

Cook Time: 40 mins

Total Time: 55 mins

Servings: 4

Ingredients:

Frittata

- 15 oz. mushrooms
- 3 oz. butter
- 6 scallions
- 1 tbsp fresh parsley
- 1 tsp salt
- ½ tsp ground black pepper
- 10 eggs
- 8 oz. shredded cheese
- 1 cup mayonnaise
- 4 oz. leafy greens

Vinaigrette

- 4 tbsp olive oil
- 1 tbsp white wine vinegar
- ½ tsp salt
- ¼ tsp ground black pepper

Directions:

1. Preheat the oven to 350°F (175°C). First, prepare the vinaigrette and set aside.

2. Slice the mushrooms anyway you like, small or big—whatever your preference.

3. Sauté the mushrooms on medium high with most of the butter until golden. Lower the heat. Save some of the butter for greasing the baking dish.

4. Chop the scallions and mix with the fried mushrooms. Add salt and pepper to taste, and mix in the parsley.

5. Mix eggs, mayonnaise and cheese in a separate bowl. Salt and pepper to taste.

6. Add the mushrooms and scallions and pour everything into a well-greased baking dish. Bake for 30–40 minutes or until the frittata turns golden and the eggs are cooked.

7. Let cool for 5 minutes and serve with leafy greens and the vinaigrette.

Nutritional Facts (Per serving):

- Calories: 1061
- Net carbs: 6g (2%)
- Fiber: 2g
- Fat: 101g (86%)
- Protein: 32g (12%)

26. BAKED CELERY ROOT WITH GORGONZOLA

Prep Time: 5 mins

Cook Time: 45 mins

Total Time: 50 mins

Servings: 4

Ingredients:

- 1 lb celery root
- 3 tbsp olive oil
- sea salt and pepper
- 3 oz. baby spinach
- 1/3 cup hazelnuts
- 3 tbsp butter
- 3 oz. mushrooms
- 1 red onion
- 5 oz. blue cheese or gorgonzola cheese or roquefort cheese, at room temperature

Directions:

1. Preheat the oven to 400°F (200°C).

2. Wash the celery root. You don't need to peel it. Cut away the roots and slice into ½-inch slices.

3. Place on a baking sheet with parchment paper. Brush olive oil on both sides and sprinkle a generous amount of sea salt on top.

4. Bake for 45 minutes, or until the celery root has turned golden brown and soft.

5. Meanwhile, cut the mushrooms and sauté in butter until golden and soft. Season with salt and pepper.

6. Roast the nuts quickly in a dry, hot frying pan, until fragrant. Let them cool slightly, and chop them coarsely.

7. Mix red onions, spinach, mushrooms and hazelnuts in a bowl.

8. Remove the baked root celery from the oven.

9. Place on plates and add the salad on top. Serve with a generous amount of blue cheese and a few drops of olive oil.

Nutritional Facts (Per serving):

- Calories: 428
- Net carbs: 13g (12%)
- Fiber: 4g
- Fat: 36g (76%)
- Protein: 12g (12%)

27. EASY AVOCADO & EGG SALAD

Prep Time: 5 mins

Cook Time: 10 mins

Total Time: 15 mins

Servings: 2

Ingredients

- 4 large eggs, free-range or organic
- 1 large avocado (200 g / 7.1 oz)
- 4 cups mixed lettuce such as lamb lettuce, arugula, etc. (120g / 4.2 oz)
- 1/2 cup soured cream or full-fat yogurt (115 g / 4.1 oz) or 1/4 cup mayonnaise (you can make your own)
- 2 cloves garlic, crushed
- 2 tsp Dijon mustard (you can make your own)
- salt and pepper to taste (I like pink Himalayan rock salt)
- Optional: chives, fresh herbs and extra virgin olive oil for garnish

Directions:

1. Start by cooking the eggs. Fill a small saucepan with water up to three quarters. Add a good pinch of salt. This will prevent the eggs from cracking. Bring to a boil. Using a spoon or hand, dip each egg in and out of the boiling water - be careful not to get burnt. This will prevent the egg from cracking as the temperature change won't be so dramatic. To get the eggs hard-boiled, you need round 10 minutes. This timing

works for large eggs. When done, remove from the heat and place in a bowl filled with cold water. I like and always use this egg timer! When the eggs are chilled, peel off the shells.

2. Make the dressing by mixing the soured cream, crushed garlic and Dijon mustard and season with salt and pepper.

3. Wash and drain the greens in a salad spinner or just by pat drying using a paper towel. Place the greens in a serving bowl and mix with the dressing. Halve, deseed, peel and slice the avocado and place on top of the greens.

4. Add the quartered eggs and season with more salt and pepper to taste. Enjoy!

Nutritional Facts (Per serving):

- Calories: 436
- Total carbs: 13.7g
- Fiber: 7.6g
- Net carbs: 6.1g
- Fat: 36.3g
- Protein: 17g

28. HALLOUMI BURGER WITH RUTABAGA FRIES

Prep Time: 30 mins

Cook Time: 30 mins

Total Time: 1 hour

Servings: 4

Ingredients:

Halloumi burger

- 15 oz. halloumi cheese
- butter or coconut oil
- 4 leaves of iceberg lettuce
- 1 tomato
- 1 avocado
- 6 tbsp sour cream
- 6 tbsp mayonnaise
- 6 tbsp ajvar relish

Cheese bread

- 4 eggs
- 1½ tbsp ground psyllium husk powder
- 2 tsp baking powder
- 2 tbsp chia seeds
- 2 cups shredded cheese

Toppings

- poppy seeds
- sea salt

Rutabaga fries

- ½ rutabaga
- 6 tbsp coconut oil

Directions:

Cheese bread

1. Preheat oven to 400°F (200°C).

2. Beat eggs fluffy, about 5 minutes.

3. Mix dry ingredients, and then blend the grated cheese with dry ingredients and the beaten eggs.

4. Let swell for about 10 minutes.

5. Put 8 piles of batter on a baking sheet and bake in the middle of the oven for 10–15 minutes until they turn nicely golden. Let cool a little before serving.

Rutabaga

1. Increase oven temperature to 450° (225°C).

2. Peel and cut the rutabaga into strips.

3. Boil for a couple of minutes in salted water. Let drain in a strainer.

4. Melt coconut oil and mix with the rutabaga in a bowl so that all strips are

covered. Sprinkle salt on the rutabaga strips.

5. Place the strips on a rack on a baking sheet. Bake in oven until golden brown on the outside and soft inside, turn once while baking. You can use a deep fryer if you have one. Rutabaga fries won't be as crispy as the potato fries as they don't contain as much starch but they taste great anyway.

Burger

1. Mix sour cream, mayonnaise and ajvar relish to make up the dressing. Let cool in refrigerator.

2. Rinse the lettuce and slice tomato and avocado.

3. Fry the halloumi cheese in butter or coconut oil until it turns a nice color and is soft.

4. Build the burger and serve.

<u>Nutritional Facts</u> (Per serving):

- Calories: 1089
- Net carbs: 5% (14g)
- Fiber: 10g
- Fat: 78 % (93g)
- Protein: 16 % (44g)

29. HIGH-PROTEIN VEGAN PUMPKIN MAC & CHEESE

Prep Time: 15 mins

Cook Time: 15 mins

Total Time: 30 mins

Servings: 4

Ingredients:

- 8 oz whole-wheat pasta or other pasta of choice
- 1 block tofu (~14 oz)
- 1 cup pumpkin purée
- 1 teaspoon each garlic powder, paprika, and turmeric
- 1 teaspoon white miso paste

Directions:

1. Add tofu, pumpkin purée, spices, and miso paste into a blender. Blend until smooth to create the "cheese" sauce. Set aside.

2. Meanwhile, boil water in a large pot. Add pasta and cook according to directions on package. Retain a small amount of the starchy pasta water. Drain pasta and return to pot.

3. Toss "cheese" sauce with pasta to coat well. Serve immediately.

<u>Nutritional Facts</u> (Per serving):

- Calories: 290
- Carbs: 49g
- Fiber: 7g
- Total Fat: 5g
- Protein: 17g

30. CRUSTLESS SPINACH CHEESE PIE

Prep Time: 2 minutes

Cook Time: 30 minutes

Total Time: 32 minutes

Servings: 8 slices

Ingredients:

- 10 ounces frozen spinach thawed, squeezed and drained (or use wilted down fresh)
- 5 eggs beaten
- 2 1/2 cups cheese any kind (I used a fiesta blend)
- 1 teaspoon dried minced onion
- 1/4 teaspoon garlic powder
- salt and pepper to taste

Directions:

1. Grease a 9-inch pie pan.

2. Combine all ingredients and pour into prepared pan.

3. Bake at 375 degrees F for about 30 minutes or until edges start to brown

Nutritional Facts (Per serving):

- Calories: 190 Calories from Fat 131% Daily Value
- Total Fat: 14.6g (22%
- Saturated Fat: 8.3g (42%)
- Sodium: 359mg (15%)
- Total Carbohydrates: 2.1g (1%)

- Dietary Fiber: 0.8g (3%)
- Sugars: 0.6g
- Protein: 13.3g (27%)

CONCLUSION

If you avoid poor quality food and stick to eating lots of fresh fruits, veggies, legumes and grains, especially whole-grains, this will provide you with almost everything you need to stay healthy. However, even veggie diets can have high levels of bad fats if they are excessive in whole dairy products, fried or fatty snack foods.

As you can see a vegetarian or vegan diet should be well thought through and planned, to ensure disease prevention and a healthy immune system.

When following a ketogenic vegetarian diet plan the key ingredient is in the planning. You should plan each of your meals to ensure that you are consuming the correct quantity of food, avoid meat-based products (such as hidden ingredients) and that each meal has the right balance of nutrients and minerals.

___<<The END>>___

Keto Diet – Reset Your Metabolism Book Series is
helpful to turn your body into fat burning machine and live healthy.

Upcoming publications

- 30 Most Delicious Ketogenic Vegan Diet Recipes

- 30 Days Plan Ketogenic Diabetic Diet

- Keto DIET for Rapid Weight Loss and Lowering Blood Sugar